DISCOVERING
FOSSILS

EXCAVATION
EXPLORATION

JESSIE ALKIRE

Checkerboard
Library

An Imprint of Abdo Publishing
abdopublishing.com

abdopublishing.com

Published by Abdo Publishing, a division of ABDO, PO Box 398166, Minneapolis, Minnesota 55439. Copyright © 2019 by Abdo Consulting Group, Inc. International copyrights reserved in all countries. No part of this book may be reproduced in any form without written permission from the publisher. Checkerboard Library™ is a trademark and logo of Abdo Publishing.

Printed in the United States of America, North Mankato, Minnesota
052018
092018

Design: Sarah DeYoung, Mighty Media, Inc.
Production: Mighty Media, Inc.
Editor: Megan Borgert-Spaniol
Design elements: Mighty Media, Inc., Shutterstock, Spoon Graphics
Cover photographs: Shutterstock, Spoon Graphics
Interior photographs: AP Images, pp. 8 (left), 9 (right), 11, 25, 29; iStockphoto, pp. 4, 9 (left), 19; Shutterstock, pp. 5 (all), 7, 13 (bottom left), 23, 27; Wellcome Collection, pp. 8 (right), 13 (right), 15, 17; Wikimedia Commons, p. 13 (top left)

Library of Congress Control Number: 2017961542

Publisher's Cataloging-in-Publication Data
Names: Alkire, Jessie, author.
Title: Discovering fossils / by Jessie Alkire.
Description: Minneapolis, Minnesota : Abdo Publishing, 2019. | Series: Excavation
       exploration | Includes online resources and index.
Identifiers: ISBN 9781532115240 (lib.bdg.) | ISBN 9781532155963 (ebook)
Subjects: LCSH: Fossils--Juvenile literature. | Animals, fossil--Juvenile literature. |
       Paleontology--Juvenile literature. | Paleontological excavations--Juvenile literature.
Classification: DDC 560--dc23

CONTENTS

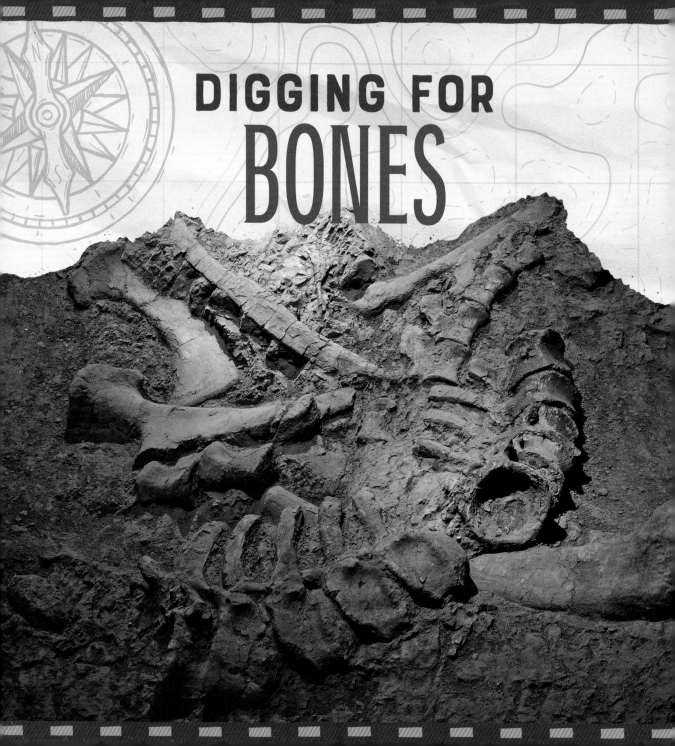

DIGGING FOR
BONES

THE SUN HAS SET ON THE QUARRY IN WHICH YOU WORK.

You have only a headlamp to see what's in front of you. Using a small **chisel**, you carefully chip away at rock. Hours have passed and you haven't found anything.

You take off your gloves and wipe sweat from your brow. You are tired but you don't take a break. You have felt a sense of excitement all day. You know a discovery is close!

You angle your chisel to the left. A chunk of rock falls away, and something catches your eye. You softly sweep away dust and dirt with a special brush. What did you find?

You keep chiseling, slowly and carefully, for days. Finally, the whole object is revealed. It's a skeleton!

The specimen is longer than your body. It has large claws and a whole set of sharp teeth. Do these fossils belong to a well-known animal? Or have you just uncovered a previously unknown species?

WHAT ARE
FOSSILS?

Fossils are the remains or traces of plants and animals. These remains are preserved in rock. Fossils can come from species that are still alive today. Others are from extinct species, such as dinosaurs!

Fossils can take several different forms. Trace fossils are records of an organism's activity. They include footprints and nests. Other fossils are the actual remains of a plant or animal. These are called body fossils.

Often, the remains of an organism decay over time. But in some cases, an impression of the organism stays in the rock. This is called a mold fossil.

Sometimes, minerals fill a mold fossil and crystalize inside it. This forms a **replica** of the organism's remains. This replica is called a cast fossil.

Rock containing fossils is worn away by water and wind. This erosion sometimes exposes fossils. Paleontologists then uncover and excavate the fossils. Paleontologists also dig at sites where they think fossils may be buried.

Fossils teach paleontologists about plants and animals from millions of years ago. This helps the scientists discover how plants and animals have changed over time. Paleontologists also learn about extinct animals such as dinosaurs and mammoths. Fossil research helps us better understand the world and its long history!

Hard pieces of animals are most likely to form fossils.
These include bones, teeth, and shells.

TIMELINE

1676

Quarry workers find the first formally recorded dinosaur fossil in Oxfordshire, England.

1795

Georges Cuvier studies the *Mosasaurus* fossil. He determines it came from an extinct species.

1824

William Buckland publishes the first scientific description of a dinosaur. He names it *Megalosaurus*.

1856

Neanderthal fossils are found in Germany's Neander Valley.

1861

A fossilized feather is found in a **quarry** in Germany. Paleontologist Hermann von Meyer names the animal it came from *Archaeopteryx*.

2006

Swedish scientist Svante Pääbo begins arranging Neanderthal **DNA** to form a full genome.

1868

Thomas Henry Huxley proposes *Archaeopteryx* could be a **transitional** form between dinosaurs and birds.

2017

Scientists in England use **CT scanning** to study Megalosaurus.

GIANT JAWS

In early civilizations, fossils were not well understood. Some ancient scholars believed fossils came from mythical creatures, such as dragons. Others understood that fossils were the remains of real organisms. Over time, experts from various fields of science contributed to theories of where fossils came from. Formal fossil collection and description began in the 1700s.

One of the first important fossil discoveries occurred in 1770 in the Netherlands. Miners found a skull that was 4 feet (1.2 m) long. It also had jaws and teeth.

The fossil was later sent to Paris, France, in 1795. French scientist Georges Cuvier thought the fossil came from a lizard species. But he realized no other known lizard species had jaws as big as the fossil's jaws. He determined the fossil, later named *Mosasaurus*, came from an extinct species. Extinction was not a popular belief at the time. But Cuvier used the Mosasaurus discovery to argue in favor of it.

Scientists believe Mosasaurus was about 50 feet (15 m) long. This fearsome creature was featured in the 2015 film *Jurassic World*.

Scientists have continued to study Mosasaurus. Today, mosasaurs are thought to have been large marine reptiles. They likely went extinct 65 million years ago. Their fossils have been found all over the world!

THE FIRST
DINOSAUR

Some of the most famous fossils have come from dinosaurs. The first formally recorded dinosaur fossil was discovered in 1676. Workers found the fossil in a limestone **quarry** in Oxfordshire, England. The fossil was a large leg bone. But at the time, no one knew that it came from a dinosaur. In fact, the term *dinosaur* did not yet exist!

Chemistry professor Robert Plot was the first to study the fossil. At first, Plot believed the bone came from an elephant. Then he thought it might be the thigh bone of a giant human! Plot published a description of the bone in 1677.

The fossil remained a mystery for more than a hundred years. Then in the early 1800s, English geologist William Buckland began studying similar bones. Buckland was collecting fossils found in Stonesfield, England. He gathered a jaw, **pelvis**, and other bones from stone quarries.

WILLIAM BUCKLAND

William Buckland was an English geologist born in 1784. In the early 1800s, Buckland explored Britain on horseback. He collected fossils from **quarries.** Buckland later created a collection of fossils, minerals, and other specimens at the Ashmolean Museum at Oxford.

In 1824, Buckland published a description of Megalosaurus, the first named dinosaur. He later traveled around Europe and gave lectures for many years. When Buckland died in 1856, he was buried in a section of limestone from the age of dinosaurs!

Buckland studied the fossils for several years. He compared them to those of other animal species. Buckland determined that the bones came from a large extinct reptile.

Buckland published a description of the creature in 1824. He called it *Megalosaurus*. This was the first scientific description of a dinosaur. However, it still wasn't called a dinosaur until nearly 20 years later.

In 1842, British scientist Richard Owen was studying Megalosaurus fossils. Owen realized they shared common features with the fossils of two other prehistoric reptiles, *Iguanodon* and *Hylaeosaurus*. He grouped these animals under the name "Dinosauria." This is where the term *dinosaur* comes from!

The discovery of Megalosaurus spurred scientists to seek out more dinosaur fossils. In the following years, many found dinosaur fossils were thought to be from

DIG THIS!

Models of Megalosaurus dinosaurs were put on display in London, England, in 1854. But early recreations often featured incorrect details, such as humps on the dinosaur's back.

Megalosaurus was 20 feet (6.1 m) long and weighed one ton (0.9 t). Scientists have determined it was a carnivore.

Megalosaurus. Over time, scientists better understood differences in the appearance of dinosaur fossils. They determined there must be many different dinosaur species. Searching for fossils became a way to discover new dinosaurs and learn about their appearance, behaviors, and more.

AMAZING
PRESERVATION

Nearly 200 years after the first recorded dinosaur fossil was found, another important discovery took place. In 1861, a fossil was found in a limestone **quarry** in Germany. The fossil was the imprint of a single feather.

No one knows who found the fossil or how it was found. German paleontologist Hermann von Meyer was the first to describe the fossil in 1861. He thought the feather came from a young bird from ancient times.

Soon after, a full-body fossil was found in the same limestone as the fossil feather. It had many features of a bird, such as feathers and wings. Von Meyer named the creature *Archaeopteryx*, meaning "ancient wing."

DIG THIS!

Archaeopteryx had light-colored feathers with black tips. This is a common pattern on birds today!

Several paleontologists studied the Archaeopteryx. But no one could agree what kind of animal it was. Was it a bird or a reptile?

A possible answer came in 1868. That year, English biologist Thomas Henry Huxley proposed the idea that dinosaurs **evolved** into birds. He thought Archaeopteryx could be a **transitional** form between the two species!

Thomas Henry Huxley observed the similarities between birds and reptiles as early as 1863.

Huxley's idea supported the theory of **evolution** presented by English scientist Charles Darwin in 1859. Evolution was not a popular idea at the time. But the discovery of Archaeopteryx supported Darwin's theory, which has since been accepted as scientific fact.

Archaeopteryx remains famous for its contribution to the study of evolution. It is also known for how well preserved its fossils are. Scientists have determined that the creature's burial conditions allowed for its perfect preservation.

Archaeopteryx lived on land near lagoons. Researchers think some of these creatures drowned in the lagoons. The animals were buried in mud deep under the water. There was little to no oxygen in these conditions. So, there weren't any bacteria to break down the Archaeopteryx remains.

Over thousands of years, the mud hardened into limestone. This captured all the tiny details of the Archaeopteryx remains. Such incredible preservation has helped paleontologists understand fossil formation. It has also made Archaeopteryx one of the most famous fossils in history.

Only 12 Archaeopteryx specimens have been found to date. But Archaeopteryx is still one of the most famous fossil species discovered in history!

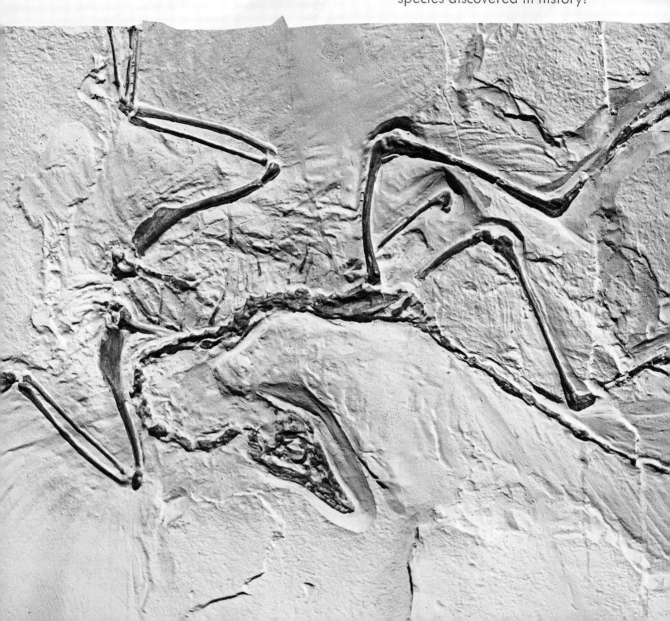

NEANDERTHAL
FOSSILS

Around the time Archaeopteryx was first discovered, scientists were studying the fossils of another important species. The fossils belonged to Neanderthals, early relatives of humans. Neanderthal fossils are some of the most-studied remains in history.

Neanderthal fossils were first found in the early 1800s in Europe. They looked like human bones. But they were shaped differently from the bones of modern humans. Some experts thought they were from humans with bone conditions such as **arthritis**.

Similar fossils were recovered in 1856. Workers found these fossils while digging in the Neander Valley in Germany. The finds included a skull and other parts of a skeleton.

The skull looked like a human's, but it had some key differences. It was oval-shaped with a low forehead. It had a thick, ridged brow that hung over the eyes. The **sinuses** and space for the brain were larger than a human's. The individuals the fossils came from were named "Neanderthals" after the valley in which they were found.

THE NEANDERTHAL SKELETON

The Neanderthal skeleton looks similar to the skeleton of a modern human. However, scientists have observed key differences.

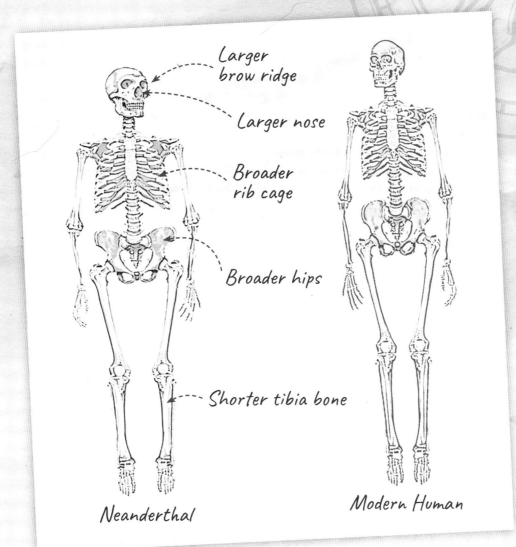

Larger brow ridge

Larger nose

Broader rib cage

Broader hips

Shorter tibia bone

Neanderthal

Modern Human

Remember, Darwin presented his theory of **evolution** in 1859. This theory and the study of Neanderthal fossils spurred scientists to explore the evolution of humans. Paleontologists began seeking out early human fossils. This led to discoveries of hundreds of Neanderthal fossils over the past 200 years.

Paleontologists have determined the age of Neanderthal fossils using radiocarbon dating. This method is based on knowledge that fossils contain carbon that breaks down over time. Radiocarbon dating measures the amount of carbon in a fossil to determine how old it is. This method has shown that Neanderthals became extinct around 30,000 years ago.

Scientists have a better understanding of Neanderthals today than when the fossils were first discovered. Researchers have determined that Neanderthals and humans evolved separately from a common ancestor. Paleontologists continue to find and study early human fossils to learn about human evolution.

DIG THIS!

Some research suggests Neanderthals matured faster than modern humans. They only lived until 30 years old on average.

Many museums display models of what Neanderthals are thought to have looked like when they were alive.

FOSSIL DNA

Advanced **technologies** have allowed paleontologists to examine fossils in new ways. One new tool is **DNA** testing. DNA testing has helped paleontologists learn more about Neanderthals and their connection to humans.

Swedish scientist Svante Pääbo began studying Neanderthal DNA in the 1990s. He **extracted** genetic material from Neanderthal fossils. In 2006, Pääbo's team began arranging Neanderthal DNA to form a full genome. They compared the results to the human genome. In doing so, Pääbo's team discovered that many modern humans have a small percentage of Neanderthal DNA!

Being able to extract fossil DNA was revolutionary to the field of paleontology. Researchers have used this technology to study the fossils of early humans, dinosaurs, and more. Scientists have even begun to extract DNA from sediment alone. This practice will help paleontologists test for DNA in places where fossils have not yet

been found. It can also help scientists learn about species without
damaging already-found fossils.

Svante Pääbo (*right*) is a director at the Max Planck Institute for
Evolutionary Anthropology in Germany. Anthropology is the study
of humans and their ancestors.

FOSSIL
FUTURE

Paleontology is much different today than it was in the 1800s. Modern tools allow scientists to study fossils without even removing them from the ground! One **technology** that allows this is **X-ray** imaging.

Scientists can use X-rays to scan rock. This produces an image of what is within the rock. In this way, X-rays can help paleontologists find and study fossils without digging. X-rays are also used to look inside excavated fossils.

In 2014, researchers in France used a new X-ray **technique** to study an Archaeopteryx fossil. The team narrowed the X-ray to the thickness of a human hair. This made it extremely powerful.

As the X-rays entered the fossil, they scattered. Researchers then created a **3-D** image of the fossil from the pattern of scattered rays. They could see tiny details of the creature's feathers and blood vessels in its bones! This technology is especially useful for studying fossils that are too bulky to scan using regular X-rays.

Researchers have long wondered whether Archaeopteryx could fly. Detailed scans of fossil wings and feathers suggest the species flapped its wings to fly short distances.

CT scanning is another powerful tool for paleontologists. A scanner rotates around a fossil. This creates a **3-D** image of the fossil. In 2017, scientists in England used CT scanning to study the Megalosaurus. They built a 3-D image of the dinosaur's jaw. The scan showed five teeth researchers had never seen before!

Paleontologists are also using 3-D printers in their research. With this tool, researchers can create model bones to build full skeletons. Scientists can also digitally reconstruct broken fossils and 3-D print new models. These 3-D fossils show scientists how an animal moved, what it ate, and more.

Such **technologies** have helped paleontologists understand the world more than ever before. But there is still much to discover about Earth's history through fossil study. With advanced technologies, scientists will continue to uncover these traces of the past!

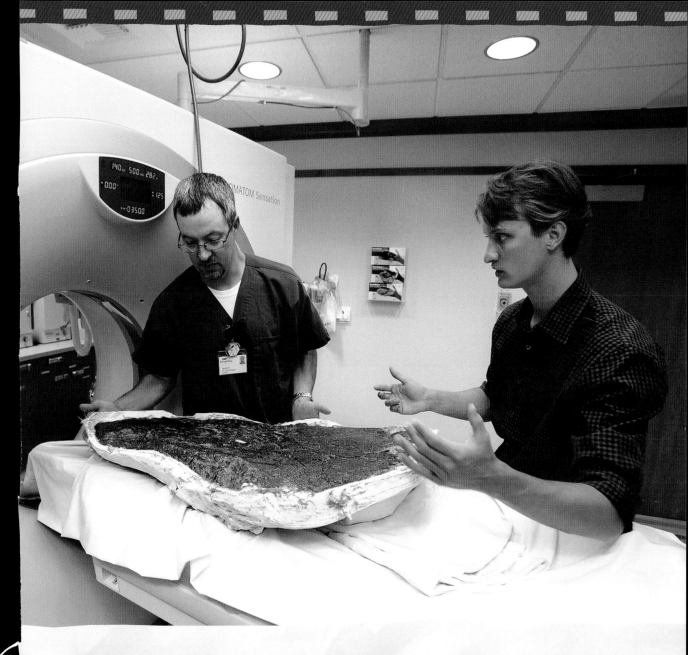

In 2013, US researchers used CT scans to examine stegosaur fossils.

GLOSSARY

arthritis — a medical condition of the joints that causes much pain.

chisel — a tool with a flat, sharp end that is used to cut and shape a solid material such as stone, wood, or metal.

CT scan — a 3-D image of an object's structure created by a combination of X-ray images.

DNA — a material in the body that helps determine what features a living thing will inherit. "DNA" stands for *deoxyribonucleic acid*.

evolve — to develop gradually. Evolution is the process of gradual development.

extract — to withdraw by a physical or chemical process.

pelvis — the wide, curved bone structure between the legs and spine of a skeleton.

quarry — a place where stone is cut or blasted out for use in building.

replica — an exact copy.

sinus — a space in the skull that connects with the nostrils.

technique (tehk-NEEK) — a method or style in which something is done.

technology (tehk-NAH-luh-jee)— a machine or piece of equipment created using science and engineering, and made to do certain tasks.

3-D — having length, width, and height. "3-D" stands for *three-dimensional*.

transitional — marked by the changing from one state or stage to another.

X-ray — an invisible and powerful light wave that can pass through solid objects.

ONLINE RESOURCES

Booklinks
NONFICTION
NETWORK
FREE! ONLINE NONFICTION RESOURCES

To learn more about fossils, visit **abdobooklinks.com**. These links are routinely monitored and updated to provide the most current information available.

INDEX